PRAISE FOR

Where Are the Snows

"Kathleen Rooney's *Where Are the Snows* is a book of investigative improvisation—interested in the loss and whereabouts of everyday goodness, the futility of contemporary politics and capitalism, the transience of joy and sorrow. Her supercharged lyrics pulse with interruption, iteration, and inference. They juxtapose absurd facts and self-deprecating queries with the timing of a standup comedian. Half heartbreaking, half hilarious, this book is 100% punk rock."

—MARCUS WICKER, AUTHOR OF *SILENCER*

"In Kathleen Rooney's *Where Are the Snows*, profound and hilarious stanzas underpin a philosophy for living in an era that feels post-claiming-to-be-post-anything. The book is both a modern pastoral with startled, awestruck observations about everything from the economy to Wednesdays and a deeply emotional elegy for a complicated, yet beloved, spirituality. Rooney's adroit use of language reveals how nostalgia and history are their own kinds of mysticism and—my favorite—that time itself is just a metaphysical joke. I mean, c'mon, her dedication reads: To the future. Rooney is at her funniest in this book, and in all the best ways: subversive, nerdy, and tragic. She writes, *You won't believe how saintly I've become. Big halo energy.* This is a great book."

—SOMMER BROWNING, AUTHOR OF *GOOD ACTORS*

"Reading Kathleen Rooney's *Where Are The Snows* is refreshing. Here is a book unafraid to face the various crises of the world and admit it might not work out. The magic of Rooney's writing is its lightness: funny, playful, cynical, indulgently dark, and poignant, *Where Are The Snows* is always delightful. I promise you won't be able to stop reading these poems."

—JOSÉ OLIVAREZ, AUTHOR OF *CITIZEN ILLEGAL*

Where Are the Snows

Where Are the Snows

Kathleen Rooney

poems

★trp

The University Press of SHSU
HUNTSVILLE, TEXAS
texasreviewpress.org

Library of Congress Cataloging-in-Publication Data
Names: Rooney, Kathleen. | Rooney, Kathleen
Title: Where are the snows : poems / Kathleen Rooney.
Description: First edition. | TRP: The University Press of SHSU, [2022]
Identifiers: LCCN 2022010681 (print) | LCCN 2022010682 (ebook)
ISBN 9781680032925 (paperback) | ISBN 9781680032932 (ebook)
Subjects: LCSH: Humanistic ethics—Poetry. | LCGFT: Poetry.
Classification: LCC PS3618.O676 W47 2022 (print)
LCC PS3618.O676 (ebook)| DDC 811/.6—dc23/eng/20220419
LC record available at https://lccn.loc.gov/2022010681
LC ebook record available at https://lccn.loc.gov/2022010682
Front cover image licensed via Shutterstock.com
Front Cover design by Bradley Ivey | Interior: PJ Carlisle
Printed and bound in the United States of America
FIRST EDITION
★trp
The University Press of SHSU
Huntsville, Texas 77341
texasreviewpress.org

In my own country I'm in a distant land
Beside the blaze I'm shivering in flames
Naked as a worm, dressed like a president
I laugh in tears and hope in despair

—*François Villon "Ballade [I die of thirst beside the fountain]"*

CONTENTS

To the future

DRESS UP

Let's give featureless time some features:

Horn-rimmed glasses—bushy eyebrows attached—and a large plastic nose above a plushy mustache.

Groucho glasses are also known as "the beaglepuss."

She who wears a disguise hard is she who tries hard.

Put the beagle of the mind in a rhinestone collar, then yank the leash. Thanks for staying on the path.

Although wearing a disguise is unlikely to fool friends, it might inspire laughter.

I never forget a face, but in your case I'll be glad to make an exception: us to the 21st century so far.

She who tries hard is she who dies hard?

Getting slapped with a stick is not actually funny.

TO REPLICATE THE SACRIFICE OF CHRIST'S JOURNEY INTO THE DESERT FOR 40 DAYS

This year I gave up hope for Lent.

The otherworldly pallor of the sky—shall we say it's greige?

Consciousness bobs—a misty blob—between optimism and nihilism.

We are under siege. We are short of sages.

It's hard to be an atheist in such an age, so why not make up your own theology?

Here, see: Before they grow up, angels are angelets, like pink piglets except with wings.

Can a fasting period make time pass faster?

Sign of the cross, sign of the times.

Sing of lying down, sing of rising.

The crux of the matter? The matter sucks.

You won't believe how saintly I've become. Big halo energy.

And Easter's still a full eighteen days away.

EVERY NOW AND THEN

Sometimes a friend posts a photo of their newborn and it's all I can do not to type, *Welcome to Hell!*

Is the fuckedness quotient really on the rise, or was it ever thus?

Sometimes I stop by the mirror and redden my lips, making myself hotter though no one can see me. Like Diana Vreeland said, "I loathe narcissism, but I approve of vanity."

One of the earliest known uses of the F-word appears in a 16th century collection of poems compiled by an Edinburgh merchant named George Bannatyne during an outbreak of plague.

Is the weather weird today? Is the sky not clear enough or is it too clear? This year feels especially endless this year.

Sometimes I sit and think, but mostly I just sit—who was it who said that? And was it always true, or only sometimes?

Sometimes I wake up and the morning light is like, *Welcome back to your absurd reality!*

What might happen if I signed my emails "derangedly" sometimes?

Sometimes I like to do things on my own, which is lucky, because sometimes the cavalry isn't coming.

Once in a while, the pigeons undulate across the blue void in such a way that I wish I could join them.

What might happen if I signed "still me, unfortunately"?

Sometimes you can get out a red pen and revise your mood. Maybe most times.

THE PRODUCTION AND CONSUMPTION OF GOODS AND SERVICES

The etymology of economy lies in household management; thrift.

I'm not into real estate fantasies, but I can see the appeal of a cottage with a slate roof, copper gutters, and period shutters. A place to shut in, shut out, shut down.

Shut up: my comeback to Mammonites demanding blood sacrifice to the death cult.

Why should I die for the economy when he would never do the same for me?

Please respect others and only take what you need: the rule on complimentary tampons and pads in the bathrooms is basically my plan for the entire economy.

The tragedy of waste. The waste of tragedy.

Can material loss yield spiritual gain? Probably so, but not automatically.

What would you make if you didn't have to make money?

I don't want to go back to business as usual. I want to give business as usual the business.

France last executed someone by guillotine in 1977.

Freeze and put your hand where I can see it! (I said that to the invisible hand of the market.)

PASTORAL

Lake Michigan churns like a washing machine today. Buckets of rain mean I remain indoors.

The distant thunder of the toilet flushing. The sky out the window a moody adolescent.

When was the last time I just sat by a tree?

Why do the woods have a neck anyway?

A week past the vernal equinox, it stays too cold for green buds or bugs.

When it comes to alcohol and cookies, why are grasshoppers minty?

Convolvulus is a gnarly name for morning glory. Ranunculus same, but for buttercups.

In Chicago, we call plastic bags blowing across the sidewalk Jewel tumbleweeds.

The wind runs up the street on invisible feet. Its breath is the shepherd, the debris its sheep.

There won't be any sunset to speak of today, but all it would have said is *Et in Arcadia ego.*

Canada geese make a V in the sky, a reminder that in the end, victory shall be theirs.

Stare too long at a screen and the heart grows pathetic: misanthropic hamster, jogging on a wheel.

Can idle merriment, nymphs and swains, ever attain on purpose what nature achieves spontaneously?

When I can't visit nature, nature visits me: the fattest sparrow on the bare ash tree.

PEDESTRIAN ACCESS

The news on the radio leads you to expect wasted landscapes. Maybe lakes of blood. But there are only puddles and mud on the sidewalk.

No need for earbuds. There's music from cars, from workmen working unseen in backyards.

You don't want to get fat; you want a stout heart.

A morning constitutional, mourning the Constitution.

Some women you pass at a fairly vast distance are at least as lovely as B movie actresses.

The blue flannel shirt of the sky fans to the horizon.

The cedar bushes in the snow look like Frosted Mini-Wheats. Babies in strollers wrapped tight as burritos. Babies in sunglasses, incognito.

What if you could tell through your toes when you entered a new zip code?

What is it that the birds are chirping from the trees? That there are no promises, no guarantees.

Undressed mannequins pose in shop windows. Dust bunnies hop the floors. Sick buildings barf their bricky entrails.

The word "jaywalk" has nothing to do with blue jays.

The human gait is called the double pendulum, and time is a virus that infects us all.

Everyone attributes that description of golf as "a good walk, spoiled" to Mark Twain, but it didn't arise until after he died. Also, you don't need golf to wreck a walk.

The hexadecimal code for "pedestrian" is 1F6B6. In XML and HTML, the string 🚶 produces 🚶. Don't send texts while you're walking. Turn off your devices. Feel what you're feeling.

Silence approaches in its gray felt cloak. Walk with it for as many blocks as possible without talking.

EPISTOLARY

Our forebears wrote hundreds of letters per year. Staring into the fire, searching for the right word. A pile of correspondence atop their desks.

My mother taught me to send paper thank-you notes.

I grew up in the suburbs. In the 90s. In the Global North. The final descent of carbon paper. Wite-Out.

During the first Iraq War, my fifth-grade class wrote letters to soldiers. I sent weekly notes with cotton socks and chocolate snacks that I'm pretty sure my pen pal mocked. He would rather I'd sent something better, like porn.

Certain return addresses feel like Pop Rocks in my heart. (You can even enclose Pop Rocks in a letter if you want.)

I just sent my friend a postcard of a place called Lonesome Lake. I've never been; I bought it in a thrift shop.

Night writes with so much black ink that it's hard to read.

Sticking international postage on an airmail letter—how long before the nations are no longer?

Probably all modern technology is at least a little bad.

No special device is required to receive a letter.

In a way, we all live on Lonesome Lake now.

That magic, though, when the envelope drops into the blue mouth of the mailbox. . . .

THE LIFE OF THE MIND

Train tracks across flat land seem infinite. But at a point not visible, they do have an end.

For Wittgenstein, concepts resemble tools and they, like tools, can cease to be useful. It isn't tragic.

Someone said to me about a photo of Audrey Hepburn, "She even looks glamorous reading." I said, "Now that you mention it, everyone looks glamorous reading."

Maybe people who dismiss style as frivolous are jealous. Who does it hurt if I flounce around in my fanciest dress?

In 1999, I read *The End of History*. But the joke's on you, Francis Fukuyama! History keeps pouring out like slurry from a factory that manufactures something besides liberal democracy.

Aporia, in rhetoric, is a useful expression of doubt.

Will professional thinkers ever abandon dialectical tensions? I doubt it.

Remind yourself daily that this is temporary.

The 22nd Century. Who can say the phrase out loud?

A friend wrote to me that in Chinese there are five seasons, not four: summer, fall, winter, spring, and the season-in-between. In English we don't have a word for that which separates after from before.

A little epistemic humility can be worth a try. The best philosophers admit they have no idea what they're talking about.

The train tracks of thought can become sclerotic. Regarding beauty reduces inflammation.

I can easily imagine the end of the world and the end of capitalism.

Can't wait to catch you on the other side, where the blank page holds its breath and waits.

HUMP DAY HAS ALWAYS BEEN A TERRIBLE NICKNAME

Today is a Wednesday. What is a Wednesday.

Every year April makes fools of us all.

Father Time pours his cornucopia.

The big dick-twirling contest is coming right up. I mean, "the election."

Justice in its purest form is not available to us.

There are more CEOs named John than there are CEOs who are women.

My condo is 1000 square feet. Pretty decent. What more do I need? I can only sleep in one bed.

Still, I look at pictures of real estate online.

Those with villas ought to share them with the villa-less. Those who are villains ought to be less villainous.

What does it mean to be between Tuesday and Thursday?

John Steinbeck wrote a sequel to *Cannery Row* and called it *Sweet Thursday*, a day he defined as falling between Lousy Wednesday and Waiting Friday. I don't know if it's worth reading, though.

Someone please recommend me some recommendations.

Living is a process of moving crisis to crisis.

I need a commendation. The littlest niceness goes the longest way.

HOW TO ACT

All the neighborhood's a stage. An open-air place for viewing spectacles and plays.

A hearse idles outside the church—I haven't seen one in a while. Rainwater drools from the mouth of a gargoyle.

Hope you like gothic flourishes and circular plots, because that's what the script calls for!

Who will play my complicated Byronic hero? With only our own eroticism to keep us warm?

I don't know how to play this scene, but the show goes on. Spiders are never too creatively blocked to weave their webs.

Is our response to any catastrophe its own disaster? Every god a jester, every jester a god.

A tableau of spirit. The rays of noon illumine the city.

The instrument I'm hoping to master here is me.

No life could be more real than this. Scarlet cardinal ad-libbing in a maple.

Is art the human response to the shock of mortality? My character lifts her middle finger. Salutes reality.

In ancient Greece, you could sit in auditoria cut into hillsides with ten thousand other people.

The critics steeple their fingers and softly say, *hmmm*.

An actor's heart rate rises the instant they have an audience.

"My first act of free will," wrote William James, "shall be to believe in free will."

Behold! Smoke from chimneys. The blackest comedy.

My longing is to perform so well that in the end I'm lashed to death by flowers from the crowd.

I search for stage directions in the airplane contrails, but the only place they lead is back to the plane.

What do I do now? Someone tell me what to do.

HUMANISTIC GEOGRAPHY

Another day, another inspirational coffee mug, poured in the kitchen, drunk in the home office: **DON'T FORGET TO BE AWESOME.** Okay. Working on it. March was the month that never ended, then it ended.

Ambivalence is the norm; that hasn't changed.

Ray Oldenburg pioneered the term "third place." If home is the first, and work is the second, the third is an informal community spot. Beauty salons and bars, coffee shops and parks. Pubs and cafes. Main streets. The post office.

I go for a walk with my morning shadow. How many places have I got these days?

Where does place end and space begin? A lodge in the wilderness is not the wilderness.

Every cozy hearth is hurtling through the cosmos.

Space is abstract; place has meaning. Like, that fence wouldn't matter to me unless you were leaning on it.

What, do I have to draw you a map?

In design school, they teach that for something to be significant it needs to exist in Vitruvian Space, centered in the intersection of desirable, feasible, viable. Which sounds even better when you say it in Latin: *venustas, utilitas, firmitas.*

I'd like to sit on the porch with you and shell peas, but I haven't got a porch, or peas, or you.

Cue the sound of wind chimes in the breeze.

I'll never stand in a driveway and hose down a sports car.

Glamour is, by definition, impractical. Could I begin to live with more extraneous detail? Placemats? Fingerbowls?

I wish we could stay in a hotel by the sea.

From up here on the third floor, it's easy to tell when the bells of St. Gertrude's shatter the glass of silence.

I wish we could prove to God above that we still loved him.

Church is a third place I never show my face in.

THE SPECIAL ORGAN OF BREATHING AND SMELLING

A tweak on the nose, a tweak of the spirit.

If you've got it, I'll sniff it—any and all of it: figs, pigs, buttered toast, compost, tallow, alley-behind-a-restaurant, kitten yawns, mown lawns, existential pains, after-it-rains, trouble, bubblegum, freedom.

Palmitic acid is the key to library scent.

I would pay through the nose for a whiff of ambergris or the musk from the glands of an actual civet.

Whenever I lose my sense of smell, I get a sensation of not quite living within the first person.

Impossible to want anyone who doesn't smell good or well.

According to Brian Eno, the secret of a good perfume "is that at the very middle, at the center of it, is a big stink. Because your nose is your most primitive sense, it's what wakes you up. It's what tells you there's a fire in the forest. It alerts you if there's a house burning down next door. Once you're awake then you can put in all the pretty smells, but not before."

Odor of the body, odor of the soul. Supposedly, Napoleon wrote to Josephine upon concluding the Italian Campaign, *I'm coming home in three days; don't bathe!*

Remember when phones could ring off the hook? Remember when phones had hooks? A comic book look. A visual sound effect. You can also draw lines to indicate smells.

Rocket ships have nose cones, but pity them for they cannot smell. A lack of smell, a berth in Hell.

Has the stable world vaporized, or did it never exist? Lucky for me, I have a keen nose for absurdity!

We don't have robust vocabularies for smells, so we borrow other images. Lemon zest smells like the squeak of a rusty door hinge. Vanilla like the treetop trill of a sparrow. Cigarette smoke is a very narrow smell. Cinnamon smells like the brightest red.

Like Basho said, "The temple bell stops— / but the sound keeps coming / out of the flowers."

THE TEN OF PENTACLES

is what the random tarot card generator dealt me today.

What's the harm in letting mysticism wrap me in its tentacles?

The courtyard of a castle. A white-haired man with two white dogs—embroidered patriarch patting his hounds. A couple with a kid around whom material abundance abounds. Surrounded by the boon of ten yellow doubloons. Said to indicate firm foundations. Said to call for a sudden windfall. Said to refer to money, not merely symbolically.

The economy, globally, has gone shambolic. Is in a shambles. What's an empire's fate but to crumble?

I might not have earned this, but that's okay, says the card.

Should I treat myself to a Butterfinger Blizzard or something?

The card states plainly: the people in the picture possess an estate. Unfair how some households do not even have a house.

Does this card mean I can help everyone who lacks bread for their repast?

One nation under a sky of five-pointed stars, silver-gilt over people who feel no guilt. What could turn a fat cat into a radical?

Interpersonal intimacy from infancy through death—that's a form of wealth.

Let's just sit quietly and admire the artwork. Don't be a jerk and tell me it's not real.

Sometimes the best action is actually inaction.

What are we going to do today? Go look at the water. Its blanket of whitecaps and mastless horizon. Go look at the past. Its forecast for the future.

In the Northern Hemisphere, it's the migration season for angels and demons. The seagulls are aghast.

A QUIET STATE AFTER SOME PERIOD OF DISTURBANCE

Deception is required for smooth social life. If anyone asks, I'll reply "Hanging in there."

Fake it till you make it is not exactly right. Harvest what helps and weed out the rest.

On earth, the best sea is the Adriatic. In space it's the Sea of Tranquility on the moon. Who wouldn't swoon for a swim in serenity?

Persistent association of calm with sinking. The fall of dusk. The mayor of a town asking protesters to settle down. A voice lowered like a pail to the bottom of a well. A dropping of temperature; an attainment of chill.

Ambition can't wait, but it'll have to learn.

First things first: stop doomsurfing the Internet.

In *The Importance of Being Earnest*, Jack says to Algernon, "How you can sit there, calmly eating muffins when we are in this horrible trouble, I can't make out."

Empty, the city's an anarchic dreamscape. Calm and eerie are different things.

A sailing ship motionless in all that calm. Windless, without agitation. The quietude of a winter evening. *All is calm, all is bright.*

Derived, most likely, from the Latin *cauma*, meaning *heat of the midday sun*, in Italy a time when everything rests.

You can't have the moral of the story without a moral code. Can you have a moral code without other people around?

Keep Calm and Carry On. Okay, but calm can actually be pretty hard to keep. A sleeping gerbil that wakes and squiggles off.

If calm were a tree it would be deciduous—shedding its leaves, putting them forth again.

I haven't been on public transportation in a while. Now even the thought of delays makes me smile. Someone come over the intercom. Someone to reassure me: *We should be moving shortly. Thank you for your patience.*

A TALISMAN ATTRACTS, AN AMULET REPELS

Humanity's been on a bit of a winless streak.

Who here believes in lucky charms? A symbol to ward. A warden to guard.

To predict a good harvest. To protect against disease.

A fetish object that objects against spells. A phylactery. A scapular. An image of an eye. A text that tells a protective secret.

A coin or a clover for wealth and health.

The Immaculate Heart of Mary above my own wary heart.

"Hail Holy Queen" is the most melodramatic prayer, and therefore my favorite: *Mother of mercy! Our Life, our sweetness, and our hope! To thee do we cry, poor banished children of Eve, to thee do we send up our sighs, mourning and weeping in this valley of tears. . . .*

I've never gotten over my childhood disappointment in finding out that rosaries are not for wearing.

I long to make a pledge to a saint or a way of life. I long to complete a rite. Would sackcloth and fasting put anything right?

I haven't got faith but I've got an aesthetic.

Evil walks among us on physical feet, and half the country is like, "Hell yeah."

Saint Michael the Archangel defeating Lucifer is a mood. *Quis ut Deus?* Who is like God?

How long has it been since I've seen any latte art in person? I'd ask for a portrait of Saint Cecilia, my confirmation name. I chose her because she loved music and died so hard.

Talisman derives from *telos* as in fulfillment, completion. In the end, it's the devotion of the wearer, not the object itself, that confers the power.

How to become a no-stats all-star, the player on the team whose presence alone causes magical outcomes?

I am ready to be initiated into the mysteries.

THE MOON IS THE MOON WHETHER WE CALL IT THAT OR NOT

Your phone is a portal, a portal to Hell. Look up. Get slapped in the face by the moon.

With a mass about 1/80th the size of the earth, the moon exposes its buttocks to the crowd.

Wiser to nature, humans of the past bestowed each month's full moon a name. Pink Moon tonight, aka Egg Moon, aka Fish Moon, aka Moon of the Sprouting Grass.

Every life seems a distant celestial body—unknowable splotches *in medias res.*

Lunation just means lunar month—the time between two successive syzygies.

Learning the names of things fills me with a feeling of profusion, like the eyes receive when they brim with a full moon.

Everybody knows about eclipses, but what about occultations? What about transits?

Moving from West to East in about 29 ½ days, the moon moons around in reverie, abstracted.

I am in awe of the facial architecture of the Man in the Moon. His bundle of thorn-twigs. His accompanying dog.

Chani Nicholas says of this evening's full moon: "Pluto brings us under the surface of things and here is where we are asked to dwell right now."

You can't have hope without futility, I guess.

"I have never known the police of any country to show an interest in lyric poetry as such," said Langston Hughes. "But when poems stop talking about the moon and begin to mention poverty, trade unions, color lines, and colonies, somebody tells the police."

We see what we have been trained to look for. Look! Twilight falls like pale blue chalk.

Carpe noctem. Seize the night.

Across the street, across the sea. It's key to have something to look forward to. Tonight, when it's 11:11, look at the clock and make a wish.

After it rises, the moon becomes a medal: a prize we receive for completing the day. But only silver. We can always do better.

THE WORD BY WHICH A PERSON OR THING IS DENOTED

I wish there were a name for the dappled glass of an old office door. Maybe there was once, and nobody knows it anymore.

Turns out, there are names for a lot of things that I thought didn't have them: epergne for *the centerpiece on a dining table.* Necrology for *an obituary or a list of deaths.*

What's the name for the breath of God in your ear?

An unseen bird calls, "Repent! Repent!" Even if I could spot it, I might not know its name.

The best names are enjoyed with the mouth and the mind.

Please write your name on the following line: _____ .
Please state your name and your occupation.

Our neighbor across the hall named her Havanese "Bob." When they go out to walk it's like she's talking to her husband.

To be good at naming, have a subtle brain.

Cold and dark as the god of the underworld, Pluto got its name in 1930, from an 11-year-old from Oxford named Venetia Burney. In 2016, when the British government allowed the public to christen their polar research ship, the most popular name was Boaty McBoatface.

I use secret permutations of my loved ones' nicknames for passwords; do any of my loved ones do the same?

Hundreds of diseases have not yet been named.

Some ancient languages had no names for numbers. Until ten thousand years ago, only about ten million people inhabited the planet, and most of those had only met a dozen or so of the others. Easier, then, probably, to remember everyone's name.

Cinder blocks are called breeze blocks if you're in the UK.

"Donald Trump" is destined to be one of the most detested names in history. In the name of all that is holy, why won't he die?

Catsup is an ugly name for a beautiful sauce: ketchup.

The use of personal names is not unique to humans. Dolphins have distinctive whistles to which they respond. Green-rumped parrotlets get names from their parents.

When dinosaurs roamed the earth, did they give each other names? And were their names as dramatic as the ones we gave them? Terrible lizards? Maximo the Titanosaur? Sue the T. Rex?

Someday no one will remember humanity's name. No one to drop a blossom on our collective grave. No grave.

Sometimes I feel an emotion that I just can't name. That's when the poop emoji comes into play.

A HUMAN FEMALE WHO HAS GIVEN BIRTH TO A BABY

A skeleton in the window of a chiropractor's office holds up a sign: **SOMEWHERE, SOMEONE THOUGHT OF YOU TODAY. AND SOMEWHERE THAT PERSON SMILED.** Was that someone my mom? Hard to say.

An infant, plump and pink as a ham, placed on the commercial grade meat slicer at the deli. The butchery of capitalism!

This is a poem that will make a lot of people hate me.

Saeva indignatio means "savage indignation," a feeling of contemptuous rage at human folly. I'm not going to let the patriarchy ride me like a horse.

No is a complete sentence and requires no explanation.

Maybe if I could be a dad, then all this would be different.

Parasitic, that phrase "women and children"—a lullaby that keeps me awake.

It would be fun to collect someone's baby teeth while pretending to be a fairy, or to tuck someone in when they're all adroop with sleep.

Mom. Mama. Mommy. Ma. Nah, I'd have my kids call me by my name.

Mommy track. Mama's boy. Mother Teresa. Old Mother Hubbard. Mother Goose. Mother lode. Mother country. Mother Earth. Mother Nature. Mother tongue. Motherfucker.

My mom used to dream of becoming an archaeologist. Dropping me off at college she said she wished that she'd never had kids. I wish I could know her as a person, just a person.

"There's no bitch on earth like a mother frightened for her kids," says Stephen King. "Mothers are all slightly insane," says J.D. Salinger.

I don't want to "mother," per se; I just want to care for others like any person should care.

"Pregnancy is barbaric," says Shulamith Firestone, and childhood is a kind of "supervised nightmare." The nuclear family is a death cult. Aunthood is my jam.

I like it when kids run around like crazy-craze and tell me they want to be paleontologists.

Mother Carey's chickens is late 18th century sailors' slang for storm petrels, or snowflakes, said to be the souls of those dead at sea.

The happiness a mother feels gazing into the faces of her children can only be matched by my happiness at having no children to gaze at. (Almost nobody believes me when I say that.)

I've run the numbers and motherhood is the mother of all raw deals.

The last word in *Moby-Dick* is *orphan*. Relatable.

TO CHERISH A DESIRE WITH ANTICIPATION

Sometimes when I wake up, I feel all right before it rushes back.

Hope in the absence of any justification for hope is Biblical. Romans 4:18: "Against all hope, Abraham in hope believed…"

We should fly the flag at half-mast all the time because so much of America is spiritually dead.

Hope implies little certainty, but suggests possibility.

The Cape of Good Hope is the legendary home of the *Flying Dutchman,* crewed by the ghosts of tormented sailors, unable to round the headland. This feels like that, except we're going to get around.

Like Saint Vincent de Paul said, "Love is inventive unto infinity."

Last October at a talk in Chicago, Patti Smith said to accept that mourning is a part of life. "Don't be afraid to feel joy in the face of sorrow or to be the bummer at a party," she said. "Every minute, I am holding a vigil," she said.

The Greek word for bird can also mean omen. Sometimes the sky is empty except for our prayers.

Remember when we were young and full of hope?

Now rain spatters the windowpane, and immense darkness lies beyond. John Prine is gone, but still on the radio. A glimmer of hope.

When somebody asks, "What gives you hope?" at first I don't know. Then I think: a house wearing a ruffle of white hydrangeas. The way the moon is in love with the sky. A golden evening, a dreaming sea, and thee.

Picture your worst fear, but with googly eyes glued on. Picture your worst fear naked wearing only black socks.

A hope, a hop, a leap in expectation. A beacon of hope. For salvation, for mercy. Tomorrow's always being born somewhere. Somebody's got to be there to catch the baby.

Could it be that persistence is our only hope for victory? Luke Perry went on 256 auditions until he got his career-making role on *Beverly Hills, 90210.*

The sunset smears honey for us to stick our dreams to.

I hope that we're all feeling better soon.

A POWER OR ABILITY OF THE KIND POSSESSED BY SUPERHEROES

If death is a specter that devours everything, then making friends with death would be a good superpower.

What if you had a superpower but it was really banal, like the ability to beat anybody in the world at checkers?

My meditation teacher, June, probably has several superpowers, but most apparent is her ability to tell without a watch when 20 minutes have elapsed.

Remember when the United States and the Soviet Union were superpowers?

You can't shame power into changing because power can't be shamed. Is America a hellbound train even Superman can't stop?

A signature look can be a superpower of sorts. Imagine Salvador Dalí without his 10-past-10 mustache. Diane von Furstenberg without her wrap dress. Malcolm X without his specs.

Who would I be now if I hadn't grown up watching *She-Ra: Princess of Power?*

The 11 Best Superpowers of All Time Ranked: X-Ray Vision, Shapeshifting, Regeneration, Invisibility, Flight, Strength, Speed, Teleportation, Telekinesis, Telepathy, Elemental Control.

Alternate List: Dark Optimism, Excelling at Small Talk, Not Sweating the Small Stuff, Jaywalking, Shattering the Tyranny of Gender, Convincing Everyone on the Planet that Black Lives Matter, Smashing the Patriarchy, Defeating Capitalism, Reversing Climate Change, Compassion, Forgiveness.

All I want is to be a tragicomic hero. Is that so wrong?

There are many heads I'd like to see tossed into a basket.

In the window of a Martial Arts studio on Sheridan Road—a prayer? A credo?—

What exists physically exists first in thought and feeling. There is no other rule. I am the creator of my experience. I am the living picture of myself. I am great. Even obstacles have a reason for being.

Just to live in a worldwide community of kindness.

I'm still a regular embarrassing person, but if you need me, I'll be over here trying to organize the chaos.

EXALTED OR WORTHY OF COMPLETE DEVOTION

A friend observes that it feels like Cloudsday, March 43rd. But today is Easter.

This morning we'll eat sweet rolls sent by my mom. Normally: oatmeal. Martin makes the best—cinnamon, molasses, and a banana stirred in until it basically vanishes. The same pot every day, with the same wooden spoon, smoothed from use, its hemisphere worn.

When it's gone, I will miss every molecule.

Outside the flowers brazenly flaunt their genitalia. Crocuses nod their purple heads like *Yes*.

They say that anyone can make a wooden spoon—all you need is a piece of wood, a knife, and desire.

Most wooden spoons are made of birch tree, beechwood, maple, or oak. Holy alliance of carved and carver.

Supposedly, ovenbirds and warblers cry, "Teach-er, teach-er!"

I am searching for some kind of holy instruction.

According to the Eastern Orthodox Church, the cross Jesus hung from was made of three woods: cedar, pine, and cypress. (Coniferous trees ill-suit utensils because of their softness and evergreen scent.)

According to everyone else, the True Cross was dogwood. God made the sturdy tree grow small and twisty, never to be used to that end again.

Why not use materials that improve with age? Trees map time, even rendered into objects.

The Catholic Church reaches out her arms to embrace her followers. I'm not a big hugger. I do click "like" on the Pope's tweet: "Dear brothers and sisters, indifference, self-centeredness, division, and forgetfulness are not words we want to hear at this time. We want to ban these words forever!"

Emotion adheres not just to objects, but objects in relation to other objects.

"You cannot do a kindness too soon, for you never know when it will be too late." Ralph Waldo Emerson said that, or something like it. Am I becoming a sentimental fool?

I must be getting old. I hope you are too.

I should go into the kitchen now. I should thank that spoon.

I'M ALWAYS UP FOR AN ARBITRARY CHALLENGE

Like *Go into your camera roll and share a photo you've taken in the past two weeks.*

On the Loyola campus, yards from the lake, a plaque that I snapped for future re-reading: **THE PROMISES OF THE SACRED HEART OF JESUS TO SAINT MARGARET MARY ALACOQUE.** A dozen oaths, like a box of spiritual donuts.

"Sinners shall find in my heart a fountain and boundless ocean of mercy." The water on the rocks forebodes total erosion. Spray flocks the clothes of fellow lake walkers.

In childhood, they say, Margaret preferred silence and prayer to play. Visions of Jesus, scourged and bloody, enduring his agony in the Garden of Gethsemane.

Am I the only one who finds Christly visitation to possess sexual aggression? You can't spell resurrection without erection. (I mean, you can, but you see what I'm getting at.)

"Tepid souls shall become fervent," and "Fervent souls shall rise speedily to great perfection."

Bursting forth from the bosom of Christ, the Sacred Heart would make quite a tattoo: shining with divine light, pierced with the lance-wound, encircled by the crown of thorns, surmounted by the cross, and bleeding.

How special to be the mystic Margaret! Jesus informing her she was his chosen instrument!

His statue in the shrine beside the plaque has arms outstretched, like "Who needs a hug?" The emptiness of his hands stands as an invitation for filling: trilling sparrows, frilly branches, small-denomination coins, sea glass. Hot dog buns for the birds to eat. Flowers at his bare and shapely feet.

James Joyce included the promises in his story "Eveline." I like Joyce all right, but he has a default meanness, the way seagulls' expressions are always mean. Has anyone ever seen a seagull without resting bitch face?

SACRED HEART OF JESUS, THY KINGDOM COME, says the carving on the base of the shrine.

CatholicOnline.com informs me I can buy a St. Margaret Mary Alacoque 14-karat gold-filled pendant for the sale price of $112.19. Sterling silver for $56.09. The Sacred Heart of Jesus shoots rays into her face, rays into the sky.

Would wearing this be a suitable display of fidelity? To say I heart danger. I heart passion. I heart intrigue.

I don't want to die in anyone's displeasure. I don't want to die.

A COURT GAME PLAYED WITH LONG-HANDLED RACKETS

Given the kind of that dork I was, badminton was my high school sport.

Everybody pictures it played casually—beer in one hand in a grand backyard—but competitive badminton is actually hard.

Music is a cosmic utterance. In the gym, we did our drills to Q101, Chicago's New Rock Alternative. *You gotta keep 'em separated. Here we are now, entertain us. I'm a loser, baby, so why don't you kill me?*

I wasn't that good.

Our coach was from China. He wasn't kidding around. We'd skip and jog, gallop and lunge for 30 minutes across the squeaking floors to improve our stamina before he'd let us pick up a racket.

Clear, drive, drop, smash, net. Forehand, backhand, universal. Footwork. Strokes. Friendship bracelets. Gatorade.

I still laugh at the word "shuttlecock."

As in many sports, there were lessons that applied off the court. Vigilance. Preparation. *Ready position! Turn, racket back!* Who doesn't want to react faster to the shot of her opponent?

The way a game can compress time is a kind of interstellar magic.

I still possess a killer serve. I reserve it these days for Streetcock—badminton in the alley—or the grass by Lake Michigan at Purple Martin Field. Birdies over the net, birds overhead: light, feathered objects aloft in the twilight.

I used to think: *If I'm not trying hard, am I even really trying?* Now I allow for the marshmallow fluff of goofing around.

My sister played, too. We still pose some trouble at doubles. To lose ourselves, when the world is stupid, in a volley swift as Cupid's arrow!

They say the game started in India and became formalized in the UK, named after a Duke's estate in Gloucestershire, but a historical link to this place has never been proved.

NASA's fleet of Earth-observing satellites monitors our planet's health from space: oceans, biospheres. They probably don't show when the Olympics get postponed.

The shuttle part of the name derives from the back-and-forth motion of the game, resembling the shuttle of a loom. Athletics as a kind of weaving together.

We shall meet again on the court of play. Or we shan't. Either way, nothing lasts forever.

ATMOSPHERIC WATER VAPOR FROZEN INTO ICE CRYSTALS

According to the original timeline, today is Tax Day.

Chicago wakes to a winter weather advisory. Whirligigs of water in solid form.

Like Prince told us, sometimes it snows in April.

An asteroid the size of a house will fly by Earth today, safely as the flakes fall beyond our windows. The astronomer in the video explained, "Space is pretty big."

One of my spouse's co-workers signed an email, "Hope Spring is eternal!"

What is the spiritual purpose of snow? Frost on the pane suggests delicacy of feeling.

Some snow spackles down like lumps of plaster. But the snow of late spring has a rarified quality. Like Swans Down cake flour, made from soft winter wheat and sifted repeatedly to be finer than all-purpose.

Scientific study says that twenty minutes of nature significantly lowers stress. The snow in the twilight, a pale blue sugar.

Ukichiro Nakaya developed a crystal morphology diagram of the diversity of snowflakes. He also made the world's first artificial snow.

The Sahara Desert was verdant at one time. Soon enough, the summer will be a swelter of melting ice pops. The globe a welter of melting ice caps.

How does snow feel about being slang for cocaine? Or a mass of static on a television screen? How does snow feel regarding snow jobs?

The birdbath with its disk of ice. Death with its ice-cold marble face. Death as phenomenon, death as concept.

What indignity to be a snowman. Peed on by dogs, head knocked off. Deliquescing.

We read "Silent Snow, Secret Snow" by Conrad Aiken in high school. "Miss Buell was saying 'Land of perpetual snow'"—and before you know it, the protagonist has gone insane: "a secret screen of snow between himself and the world." It gets classified as horror, but it sounds okay.

Snowbank, snowball, snowbird, snow-blind. A blizzard makes everybody look ambiguous, like angels.

O, heights of ecstasy! O, throes of despair! Emotion is not a state but a process. In that sense every person creates their own weather.

Snow me under. Wake me when it's over. (But I know, I know. It's never over.)

EKPHRASTIC

When the museum is closed, is it still a museum?

Humans illumine a room with a glow.

What's an exhibitionist without a voyeur? What are we, any of us, but objects in limbo?

Peter Schjeldahl pronounces art "inoperative without the physical presence of attentive viewers."

"Museum" as in "seat of the Muses." As in "place of learned occupation." As in often imitated and often duplicated. Temples to necromancy: communion with the dead.

According to his friend Harry Torczyner, Magritte encouraged the reproduction of his paintings, mechanical or otherwise, because he "disliked the orthodox, conformist notion of the unique *exemplum*." I love Magritte, but I kind of disagree. Being inside a gallery is just really sexy.

A picture is worth a thousand words—hard to think of a sillier saying. Dorothea Lange herself believed "there is no photograph that cannot be fortified by words."

How much does a viewer need to know about art? Is gut impulse enough? Some paintings evoke an instinctive sadness. The people who ground these colors all rest in the ground.

Sorry, but that Foucault essay about Velázquez's *Las Meninas* that everybody adores? It's unreadably boring. Whereas the painting itself? Eloquence of high order.

Encaustics. Potteries. Etchings. Fabrics. I'm most impressed when an oil painting or sculpture resembles the thing it's trying to look like. Cooler palettes for winter. Convincing effects of daylight.

To collect is different than to create, although collecting can be creative.

Lately, I can't stop thinking of Tiepolo's painting of a fat Baby Jesus brandishing a bird, chubby hands to be stabbed by future nails. The composition suggests a theory of mercy. *Madonna of the Goldfinch*, c. 1770. Please google it. I'll wait.

Raphael's version in the Uffizi is more famous, but I like it less. Tiepolo's hangs in the National Gallery in DC. How much does that matter? Both hang around the internet.

According to legend, the goldfinch acquired its spot of red when it plucked a thorn from Christ's head during His ascent to Calvary. Plopped in the face with a drop of His blood!

Is the *Depressed Pigeon* meme art? Is any meme, however obscure or fashionable? What is the symbol of our future Passion?

How sorry I am about your suffering! the goldfinch's eyes seem to gleam through her silence. Eradicating its cause is beyond her power. But she's with you.

FORETELLING THE FUTURE BY A RANDOMLY CHOSEN PASSAGE FROM A BOOK

Look! More snow, only slightly cold, and I'm alone inside with my hissing radiators.

An "office" sounds better if you call it a "study."

A perfect morning for some bibliomancy.

Turn to the first poetry book you see, an exclusively online friend of mine tells me. *On the page of your birth month, use a word from the title to write your first line and improvise from there.*

I like to think I know my own mind, and my own mind likes a little outside guidance.

Chinese Erotic Poems from the Everyman Library, though I am a woman, and the libraries are closed. "The Riverbank," anonymous, 600 BCE: "By the high riverbank / I cut branches and twigs. / When I don't see my man, / I feel morning-ravenous." Pretty spicy.

Whenever I walk into a library I wonder: how many of these books have been used to kill spiders?

Weeping willows by a riverbank toss their long hair. Theirs is the most lyrical tree name, am I right?

Linnaeus believed them to be in Psalm 137: "By the waters of Babylon, there we sat down and wept, when we remembered Zion / On the willows there we hung up our lyres. . . ."

Who will write the moral history of my generation? Divination. A divine nation.

(Turns out willows don't grow on the banks of the Euphrates. Turns out they were poplars.)

Unpopular opinion alert: asking advice does not oblige you to take it.

Robert Browning chose Cerutti's *Italian Grammar* to learn the fate of his relationship with Elizabeth Barrett. How dry! But then, this translation exercise: "If we love in the other world as we do in this, I shall love thee to eternity."

The world is way too goddamn with me. I'm trying to be present to the spatiotemporal qualities of this cup of coffee.

A pregnant pause—what will it birth? With nowhere to go, lounging around eating candy, time just gets fatter. As though in confinement.

Quick! Somebody give me another assignment. Somebody tell me that what we do matters.

THE STATE OR PERIOD OF BEING A CHILD

This morning my sister sent a recording of my nephew, five years old, standing on a stepstool at the kitchen stove: "Please enjoy this video of Luka watching popcorn pop. Little pleasures I guess!" I watched it five times in a row without stopping.

One of my favorite prompts to give to my students: *Pick a scene from your childhood and describe it in three sentences. Long shot, middle shot, close-up. Gradually zoom us in, really letting us see it.* Fascinating how other people depict their youth. Misty naturalism? Horror-movie fisheye?

In their classic book on fairy tales, Iona and Peter Opie write, "a man not given to speculation might as well walk on four legs as on two. A child who does not feel wonder is but an inlet for apple pie."

What do I remember the most about childhood? An intense and often thwarted desire to be understood. Also struggling not to laugh with my sister in church, mint chocolate chip ice cream in pale green scoops, and calling milk "moo juice."

How do kids acquire their shared body of folklore? Wherefore all of us at Humphrey Daycare Center in Shreveport disporting in the playground to the dirty rhyme: *There's a place in France / where the naked ladies dance / There's a hole in the wall / where the men can see it all*?

Child abuse, child molester, child care, child's play.

The concept of childhood didn't emerge in Europe until the 1600s. The birthday party didn't start until the mid-nineteenth century.

Miss me with your gauzy nonsense about carefree innocence.

Every dad a glass tyrant, afraid to shatter. No truck with pluck or smarts or suggestions. Just a shush from mom. Just a fatherly slap in the face for lip and sass.

Childhood and its irrevocability. Childhood and its vulnerability. The ability to feel deeply rubbed away by something referred to as maturity.

Geographies of childhood! Riding bikes around the neighborhood until you enter the suburbs of adulthood. Before you know it, that's where you have to live.

Parenthood? Hard pass. I never asked to be born.

"Anybody who has survived his childhood has enough information about life to last him the rest of his days," said Flannery O'Connor. She portrayed herself as "a pigeon-toed child with a receding chin and a you-leave-me-alone-or-I'll-bite-you complex."

How much is enough to pronounce an experience good?

The suffix "-hood" denoting "state, condition, character, etc." or a body of persons of a particular class. The quandary of quantifying that which is qualitative.

What's the statistical probability of possessing "a happy childhood?"

A BUILDING THAT SERVES AS LIVING QUARTERS

Sometimes you hunt the house, sometimes the house hunts you.

A shelter or refuge, a den or a nest. One of twelve sectors into which the celestial sphere is cleft. What kind of house is best for a Pisces? Asking for me.

A full house on opening night. It's on the house. Head of household. A transitive verb where you house your guests. Don't forget to put on some pants before leaving the house.

Our houses of government ought to be placed under house arrest until they repair the nation that houses us.

Where I warehouse my books. Where I sniff the whiff of pancakes on the morning air. Where seclusion seduces like an unreliable suitor. Seclusion sounds sexy; reclusion like a hex.

Cities used to be walled for protection. If honeybees possess a notion of home, it probably involves hexagonal patterns.

I'd love for you to come to my house for dinner. I spent the weekend puttering around the house. Strictly speaking it's a condo.

A solarium can be a cube of sunshine and enlightenment, like living inside a Funfetti cake.

My one regret at not having a yard is that there's nowhere to erect a statue of Saint Francis, basically a socialist and an environmentalist.

Is the house the body and the person the mind? No, because the house has a mind of its own. Units of physical infrastructure alone do not houses make.

I took Shop, not Home Ec, but I'm a pretty good cook.

Barefoot Saint Francis, preaching a sermon to birds, pigeons under an oak tree like so many angels, his words emerging from the door of his lips. *Praised be You, my Lord, through Sister Mother Earth, who sustains us and governs us and who produces varied fruits with colored flowers and herbs.* In the 13th century he said this.

Make yourself at home. Nothing to write home about. It gives me home-field advantage.

Houses are made with analog tools. Is prayer the most analog mode of communication? Hang a crucifix on the wall, and boom! Your room is a house of worship. *God, please fix this*: the simplest request.

House as means of self-expression. A reverie of roses. A shivery enclosure. A southern exposure. Some houseplants. A sign in a window, trying very hard: **EVERY DAY MAY NOT BE GOOD, BUT THERE'S SOMETHING GOOD IN EVERY DAY**, it says.

The room where you rest, the room where you dream. The room where even things assembled to defy meaning cause you to work to make them mean. Where colorless green ideas sleep furiously. Where the vertebral silence indisposes the licit sail, the curtains blowing in and out with the breeze.

Where the creaks traverse the floor like choreographed dancers.

Have we set our house in order? The most effective questions have several right answers.

TO CELEBRATE THE ANNIVERSARY OF SOMEONE'S BIRTH

At first birthdays were reserved for kings and saints. But it's rainbow sprinkles and face painting for everybody these days.

The best way to avoid having your birthday ruined is to avoid having any expectations for your birthday.

Without the delineation of years, time would become an expanse of open water. Horizonless, shark-filled. One of my biggest fears.

A rush of Orange Crush—that sparkle on the tongue—and "Make a wish!" shouted at the top of tiny lungs are a couple of things I recall. Balloons and streamers and the first piece of cake. Conical hats with elastic chinstraps.

Is a birthday party an instance of what Durkheim meant by *collective effervescence*? Profane tasks cast away for a sacred second?

Whence my ambivalence about birth as metaphor? Birth for entities not brought forth from a womb?

"Happy Birthday to You" is a bit of a dirge.

It's said that the party hat may originate with the dunce cap. An abrogation of social norms? Not punishment in school, but foolish cavorting. Worn for the pinning of tails on donkeys. The tossing of eggs. Sported for a sack race.

Don't say "a star is born" unless you're talking about the movie. Don't tell a woman her books are her babies.

For my next birthday, please remember that I love getting mail. You could send me a funny card, and maybe a package, a package full of money. Or a necklace made of lapis lazuli, believed by the ancients to ward off melancholy.

What an ego boost, to have one's birthday suit evaluated by another person as cute.

"Today is the oldest you've ever been, and the youngest you'll ever be again." Supposedly Eleanor Roosevelt said that.

I wouldn't say I have a problem with mortality. If anything, I tend to gravitate toward the timeworn: a neighborhood where the roots of the trees crack the sidewalks.

Birthdays are about pleasure—excess and decadence. But pleasure is painful. Because memento mori. Because hoary cliché: we're not getting any younger.

The candles gutter; the candles go out. Better to blow them dark yourself.

Birthdays are okay, but what about deathdays? Of the 365 we cycle through annually, on one of them, we'll cease to be alive.

Should the hour of arrival be more of a factor? Should some of us have birthnights?

Mayonnaise is my favorite secret ingredient for cake, birthday or otherwise.

There's no predicting the days of greatest significance. Best simply to be vigilant. Like my friend Beth said, not even trying to be wise, "In my life, the piñatas come around pretty quick—I just swing at them with my stick."

THE PHYSICAL UNIVERSE BEYOND THE EARTH'S ATMOSPHERE

Astrophysicists announced today that they've detected gravitational waves resonating at the perfect frequency to harmonize with a song by Elvis Presley. "Can't Help Falling in Love" sung by a pair of orbiting black holes.

The space fascination gene—I used to think I lacked it.

Probably I was afraid. Space is so big! Eerie as a library that appears to have no patrons. (Or maybe they're all hiding.)

Black hole as home for the Holy Ghost? Holey ghost. Wholly ghost.

Belinda Carlisle sang that heaven is a place on Earth, but half our nation would prefer to make it hell.

People who've been say that space has a burning-metal smell.

The crew of Apollo 17 snapped the Blue Marble in 1972. A marvel. Its meaning simultaneously clear but mysterious.

Is space really the final frontier? Space cowboys flying around high on their own supply?

Frederick Jackson Turner said, "American democracy was born of no theorist's dream; it was not carried in the *Susan Constant* to Virginia, nor in the *Mayflower* to Plymouth. It came out of the American forest, and it gained new strength each time it touched a new frontier." Such theories make me want to shriek into the ether, "Everybody, look out!"

As Ridley Scott said, in space, no one can hear you scream.

Astronauts experience the Overview Effect—the sudden perception of the delicacy of our planet. "From out there," said Edgar Mitchell, sixth man to walk on the moon, "international politics look so petty. You want to grab a politician by the scruff of the neck and drag him a quarter of a million miles out and say, 'Look at that, you son of a bitch.'"

One of my students told me that 7% of the total population of humans who ever lived are alive today. Another said that at any given time 8% of the people in America are in a Walmart or on their way to or from one.

According to howmanypeopleareinspacerightnow.com, there are three: two Russians and one American.

"Astronauts" are "star sailors"; "cosmonauts" sail the universe. Either becomes well-versed in the stellar depths.

Wanna have your mind blown a little bit apart? Space is only an hour away if your car could drive straight up.

When she was five, my niece arrived at a cosmic understanding: "We're *on* the Earth, but we're *in* space." Holding my hand in the backyard at twilight, repeating it thrice lest it not get through my head.

They say in heaven, love comes first. Wise men say only fools rush in. Though it seems empty as a catacomb, for all we know, space is full of beings speaking to each other in what can only sound to us like code, and the footsteps of angels unafraid to tread.

THE POINT IN TIME OR SPACE AT WHICH SOMETHING ORIGINATES

Don't picture the bottom of the hill; imagine the top. The effervescent thrill of making a start. That little *psshhttt* moment when you open a pop.

Whence the superfluity of the expression "a new beginning"? The insistence of the speaker? A pep talk to the self?

"In the beginning God created the heaven and the earth. And the earth was without form, and void; and darkness was upon the face of the deep. And the Spirit of God moved upon the face of the waters." As books go, the Bible is pretty uneven. But what a beginning!

New money, new car, new baby, new wife. Waking up a new person. Starting a new life.

Tonight it's a New Moon. As the moon moves between the earth and the sun, the far side of the lunar surface will be illuminated, but no one on earth will see anything of it.

In *The Nature of Things*, in 45 BCE, Lucretius wrote, "All life is a struggle in the dark." Go around saying things like that and you'll literally never be wrong.

To be alive is to feel as though we all arrived late and missed the beginning of the movie.

The beginning of the book. The beginning of the month. It was clear from the beginning that we'd never win. Nobody remembers the beginning of the feud.

When the moon is new, the sky is extra-dark (like the best kind of chocolate), slivered by only the skinniest crescent.

New Orleans, New Zealand, New Mexico, New England—pure unoriginality? Or an attempt to improve reality—to claim some of the traits of home, only better? New America, anyone?

Sorry to say it takes more than 21 days to form a new habit. That's just a myth that became accepted as fact. Then again, with a bad behavior, one or two repetitions is probably enough when it comes to doing drugs or eating a donut.

"Could the young but realize how soon they will become mere walking bundles of habits, they would give more heed to their conduct while in the plastic state." So said William James.

A gallant habit to cultivate is using less plastic.

People like to conceive of narrative as an arc, but arcs are retrospective, not reflective of incidents as they were happening. Experientially speaking, it's a perpetual present.

Can beginner's luck apply from moment to moment? Not sure, but I hope so.

I don't like the Beatles, but "Tomorrow Never Knows" is a good song. "All play the game Existence to the end"—pause—"of the beginning." Whoa.

THE SURROUNDINGS IN WHICH AN ANIMAL OR PLANT LIVES OR OPERATES

April feels crueler than usual this year.

Yesterday was the 50th anniversary of Earth Day. Four and a half billion years ago, the planet's birthday happened, but in what month we'll never know.

Three days ago marked the 10th anniversary of the BP Deepwater Horizon Oil Spill. How long until the next despoilment?

Earth is the solid footing formed of soil. Earth is the sphere of mortal life, as distinguished from the spheres of spirits.

Inaccurate to claim that "humans are the real virus." But fair to say some of us are the scum of the earth.

In March, a false tweet about dolphins returning to the formerly squalid canals of Venice got 40,000 likes. "Nature just hit the reset button on us," typed some guy.

Nice try, but humans constitute and are constituted by nature. Animals all, we do not stand apart. There is no away, there is no outside.

The virus is as thin as one-thousandth the width of an eyelash. A human eyelash, we mean, relating everything always to us.

My friend Sarah's mom sent her a lamb cake over Easter. "I thought it would be made of ground up lamb," she emailed me. "Really, it's a very cute lamb-shaped vanilla cake with coconut frosting."

The prospect of killing animals ought to be more disgusting.

In his essay "Bad News," John Berger wrote, "Compassion need not be written with capital letters. It simply involves a recognition of losses which are not, at the first degree, one's own."

On a walk last week, we saw a bird smushed on the asphalt in the crosswalk. Looked it up in the Cornell ornithology app. A hermit thrush. Whose fault the window? Whose fault the crash?

I don't know if people who've never seen them can comprehend how great the Great Lakes are. Tapestries of sky and beach. Lake Michigan thrashing the sand, a Midwestern Ocean.

When Saint Jerome was living out in the boondocks, he tamed the King of Beasts by pulling a thorn from its paw. Every medieval rendering—fleshy hand upon feline claw—reveals tenderness, as well as the fact that the painter had probably never seen a real lion.

Until not too many centuries ago, people still believed in the existence of unicorns: white, horse-like, tameable by a virgin. Marco Polo claimed this image was all wrong. Actual unicorns were black and ill-tempered, enormous and ugly. (What he'd seen turned out to have been a rhinoceros.)

A fall to earth. A massive earthquake. What on earth is going to happen next?

Bernard-Henri Lévy tweeted that the coronavirus was not a black swan but a gray rhinoceros. The difference, he said: "The second was predictable, announced, but, like the ostriches we put our heads in the sand and we didn't want to listen." Ostriches don't really behave that way, but point taken.

Despicable, that concept we call "the apocalypse"—too neat, too total. At best, the end of the world gives us a lick and a promise. Like us, it's an animal that likes to play with its food.

THE ACT OF PASSING ACROSS OR THROUGH

Who would have guessed that I'd miss the bus? Not like, at the stop, but riding it at all. As in, who would have guessed that I'd miss the bus this much?

I used to have a 45-minute commute by the CTA. Now it's a 20-second hop from bedroom to office.

Yesterday, on a walk, I saw a couple waiting on Broadway, and a standard 40-footer just blasted past them. Another passerby asked them, "Why aren't you mad?" and they explained the new rules: no more than 15 riders at a time, or 22 on the 60-foot accordion-style articulated ones.

Fewer people now bus dishes, bus tables.

My nephew, who is five, believes that riding the subway is the funnest activity you can do in a city. I'm not sure he's wrong.

A busman's holiday means leisure time spent doing what one does for a living, like when London bus drivers ride the buses on their own days off.

That flicker like a filmstrip when one train passes another in the subway!

Pascal conceived the first bus service in 1661. A fleet of coaches, he said, should "circulate along predetermined routes in Paris at regular intervals regardless of the number of people," picking up passengers for a low fixed fare.

Fair to say mass transit is a kind of miracle.

Bus is short for *omnibus*, which means "for everyone."

Riding the Brown Line at twilight, gazing right into an infinity of windows. The slowest rollercoaster. The coyest voyeurs.

What could we enjoy if we weren't ruining things for ourselves?

The stacked romance of the double-decker bus. The peculiar hierarchies and rules of the school bus.

Who would you most like to throw under the bus?

To choose to be a passenger rather than a driver is to check a box marked Existential Freedom.

Reading demands undistracted progress, and there's something unbeatable about reading on rapid transit.

Pascal also thought humans bet with their lives that God exists or not. "Reason cannot decide between the two alternatives," he said. "You must wager (it is not optional)." But: "if you gain, you gain all; and if you lose, you lose nothing."

Sometimes the wait for the bus is so long, it feels like an exercise in probability theory.

The smell of mass transit: a gruesome perfume.

If I saw Pascal on the bus, I'd try to talk to him.

THE SWEET AND FLESHY PRODUCT OF A TREE OR OTHER PLANT

My sixth-grade teacher's grandmother held a grudge against bananas. When she emigrated from Poland, someone at Ellis Island handed her one but didn't show her how to eat it. She choked the whole thing down, peel and all.

What kind of fruit makes the best filling for a pie graph? Globally, only 55 percent of people live in countries with adequate availability to meet the five servings of fruits and vegetables daily.

Growing up, I loved the fruit pizza in the buffet at the Nebraska chain Valentino's. The dough was just dough, but the sauce was icing, and the toppings were blueberry jam and little pebbles of streusel.

I heard on the radio that if we all ate enough fruits and vegetables, there'd be huge shortages. Diets are responsible for more deaths than smoking. People are simultaneously overweight and malnourished.

It can take quite a while for an idea to bear fruit.

Canning rarely improves what's canned, but fruit can be an exception. How the grapes in fruit cocktail bob like slimy eyeballs. How happily I would eat them all.

In English, the color orange is named after the fruit, which didn't arrive until the 1500s. Chaucer wrote about Chanticleer the Rooster dreaming of a fox invading the barnyard whose "color was betwixe yelow and reed," mixing the color as a painter might.

We were standing in a kitchen, chopping up pineapple, when my friend Eileen turned to me and said with vehemence, "I hate it when somebody only eats a *little bit* of fruit."

My spouse's boss refuses to eat fruit because "It squirts in your mouth."

My favorite fruits are the ones for which seasons still matter. Good luck getting a ripe fig in Chicago in January. Fuck the expectation that you should be able to.

A tomato is technically a fruit but functionally a vegetable. Rhubarb is technically a vegetable but functionally a fruit. I don't find pedants particularly cute.

The "Hail Mary" is an otherwise beautiful prayer, but the line "Blessed is the fruit of thy womb, Jesus," feels cringey. Then again, a fruit is the ripened ovary of a flower with its included seeds, so more than likely the problem is me.

Fruit of the Loom is a decent name for a company, and a pretty good Bible joke.

The metaphors of business-speak are vacuous, but literal low-hanging fruit is fun to pick.

A grape vine takes five years to harvest, an apple tree six to ten, an avocado as long as fifteen.

Holy Mary, Mother of God, pray for us sinners, now and at the hour of our death. Amen.

When life gives you bananas, make banana bread.

When agriculture collapses, fruit is what I'll miss the most.

Is Jesus the last fruit I should think of before I'm dead?

A PLACE SET ASIDE FOR BURIAL OF THE DEAD

Alone in a graveyard I feel like Medusa, everyone around me turned into stone.

Nowhere's more peaceful than a cemetery to stroll. The dead pose no threat, and technically every walk heads graveward.

Rosehill Cemetery is the largest in Chicago, its beautiful name the result of a typo. It was supposed to be Roe's Hill, after a local farmer who refused to sell his property until the city promised to name the boneyard in his honor. It contains 350 soldiers killed in the Civil War and 61 victims of the Iroquois Theatre Fire and a lot of dead from other tragedies that nobody remembers.

Open the book of nature and read. Lichen on granite. The sheltering trees. A few brown leaves, raspy as pencil shavings. Woodsmoke drifting from somebody's chimney.

My sculptor friend who lives in Rome wrote me: "I have a small collection of human bones that date back to when I used to study anatomy." He plans to bury them in the vacant lot next to his studio if anyone decides to develop it, in the hopes the resulting investigation would hold up construction.

Cemetery from the Greek for *sleeping place.*

"Tireless" people are often quite exhausted.

The deer here seem to hold the dead very dear, grazing near headstones to leave the carvings clear. The cottontails hop softly, as if they know beneath their feet are the ceilings of the deceased.

Morbid to have a fave grave? Maybe. Anyway, mine is Lulu Fellows, dead of typhoid at 16 in 1883. **MANY HOPES LIE BURIED HERE,** says the engraving at the base of a life-sized statue, encased in glass, of Lulu reading, book in lap.

As a kid, I gravitated to St. Mary's Cemetery in Hubbard, Nebraska, on a bluff south of the town of 300 souls. Packed with Rooneys. More dead people than live ones. A few tall pines, dying like Dakota County was dying. It felt incredibly remote, but wasn't even a mile. Across Pigeon Creek, not far from the reservoir.

There was another one called Epidemic Cemetery, but you needed permission to hike there. High on a hill above Highway 35, it began during a diphtheria outbreak and housed mostly kids.

Better by far to travel than arrive. Because what's the point of anything when it all ends up here?

Necropolis. God's acre. Potter's field. I would like my headstone to read **DEAD TO PERFECTION.**

I used to hold my breath when passing a cemetery, lest I inhale the spirit of someone recently dead. Now I march right in and breathe as deeply as I can.

In the year 2000, the meaning of life was sold on eBay for $3.26.

Graveyards tend to generate generational thinking. If only I could be a grandparent without being a parent.

Saint Vincent de Paul wrote in a letter to his friend Claude Dufour, "Alas! Monsieur, there is no lot in life where there is nothing to be endured." That was in March of 1647.

Graveyard shifts. Shifts in perspective.

Like Carl Sagan said, the pale blue dot of Earth and everyone on it—every young couple in love and all the rivers of blood—are no more than a mote of dust suspended in a sunbeam.

Meaningless suffering is the aim of Satan.

Guess we'd better find some meaning.

ONE AUTHORIZED TO PERFORM THE SACRED RITES

Like gold brocade on a priestly garment, ritual renders the everyday festive.

I might still be Catholic if they let women be priests. I might still be Catholic if they let *me* be a priest.

My Granny Marie was one of six kids, two thirds of whom took religious orders. Her sister Elizabeth became a Sister, and all but one of her brothers went into the priesthood: Father Fran, Father Henry, and Bishop Alfredo. Faith of a kind most people never witness in person, let alone know in their souls.

My childhood parish, St. Scholastica, was named for the patroness of book fairs. But altar girls were not welcome there until I was too old. A sign on the tree house: **NO GIRLS ALLOWED.**

Some posit *priest* comes from the Latin *praepositus*, person placed in charge. The language of the conquerors becomes "the" language.

Who wouldn't want the opportunities for advancement? To don the vestments? To grant the sacraments, especially penance?

Being a nun seems like zero fun.

I am not trying to be offensive.

Examination of Conscience: not the best quality, but I'm pretty all-or-nothing.

There is no system that a clever person with bad intentions can't abuse.

No finer line between beauty and kitsch than you find in Catholicism. To wit: the pale pink crucifix that hung above my girlhood bed, which used to belong to my mom, affixed with the glow-in-the-dark body of Jesus.

The feminine noun *priestess* wasn't coined until the 17th century to refer to female presiders over the religions of antiquity. Even then, many of them had to perform sacred prostitution.

Outside now in the gray daylight, life and death do-si-do as usual. Faith makes the facts less maddeningly casual.

A little less agog, a little more ecstatic. Less "Oh My God" and more "O My God!"

Prester John was a legendary medieval king and priest, said to rule over the Far East when the Christian West was militarily threatened and culturally backwards. Who doesn't dream of a mythical deliverer?

We should be searching for a priest who can perform an exorcism on America.

Priest's crown is another name for dandelion. *Priest hole* sounds dirty, but only means a secret room or place of concealment for a priest (as in an English house during the Reformation).

Who doesn't want this grim slog to be going somewhere?

During the Enlightenment, *priestcraft* took on the pejorative sense of "arts and devices of ambitious priests for attaining and holding temporal power and social control."

Growing up, there was always a priest around when we needed one. When my parents bought a new car, Fran or Henry would bless it with holy water. A birthday? Holy water. Saying goodbye after dinner? Holy water.

Forget calling my Senator; I would like to dictate policy requests directly to God.

The legend of Pope Joan: a learnèd woman who disguised herself as a man and ascended the papal throne, eventually exposed by giving birth during a procession. I got in trouble for even talking about it.

In Sunday School, aka CCD, we gazed at religious paintings. One-point perspective makes faraway objects recede.

How long before we walk through the pearly gates of peace? No more Satan's spawn spouting nonsense on TV. A heavenly jukebox ready to play everybody's favorite song.

My faith remains gone. And yet my ears strain. A longing to hear someone in the beyond explaining: *Follow the sound of my voice. Rejoice when you get to the end of this hallway.*

A SOURCE OF INSPIRATION, A GUIDING GENIUS

A male muse walks into a bar. Punches the time clock. Strikes a pose.

Seriously, though. Is there a term for male muses? A search of the internet reveals: no.

The original nine were inspirational goddesses, daughters of Zeus and Mnemosyne, aka Memory.

Some words are to be preferred not as nouns but as verbs: "The writer's beloved wife was his muse" versus "I could sell the house, she mused, but then where would I go?"

Nobody asked me to do this. I just wanted to.

It takes a lot longer than five seconds to muse.

Beauty can help but isn't required. Golden everlastings and parasol pines. A dusty trail. A fine view of the sea. Some bees.

When I think "thought," do I mean the content of the thought? Either way, I don't think "inspiration" arrives from "outside."

According to philologists Diez and Skeat, "to muse" derives from "to stand with one's nose in the air."

The myth of the tortured artist—it shimmers with glamour. But why would you care to be known as vain and unreliable?

Caravaggio once drew his sword on a waiter who served him artichokes in butter instead of oil. Like, who does that?

Plato, probably, is the one to blame, with his idea of divine madness—a visit from above that lets an artist create. If the local plumber acts up he's just being a dumbass, whereas when an artist does the dumbassery, it gets glorified as his essence.

Shelley, Byron, Poe—what a pack of assholes. (Keeping the list short here for the sake of time.)

Yeats wrote, "The intellect of man is forced to choose / Perfection of the life, or of the work, / And if it take the second must refuse / A heavenly mansion, raging in the dark." I call bullshit.

Killing old lies is like trying to whack mosquitoes with a tennis racket.

Knowing all the muses comes in handy doing crosswords.

I'll admit to craving an external catalyzer sometimes. Something to yank the me out of me.

As a teacher, I believe that the best is already in everyone, and my job is mostly to draw it out.

I did this because I wanted to, not because I had to. Not because anyone made me. That's different than saying that nobody helped.

UBI SUNT

The clock radio woke me with that Chad & Jeremy song: *That was yesterday and yesterday's gone.* Appropriate, I suppose, but a little on the nose.

It rained heavily yesterday afternoon. I mailed the letter yesterday.

I'm jealous of the poet François Villon. First, because he no longer has to mess with anything here, being dead. Second, of his line, "But where are the snows of yesteryear?"

Rhetorically, colloquially, life passes quickly.

Is that today's paper? No, it's yesterday's.

These songs are part of all our yesterdays, but nobody's interested in yesterday's pop stars.

I read yesterday that Iceland won't be killing any whales this year. Workers need to be in close proximity to hunt the whales and process the meat.

It's been over a year, but it seems like only yesterday that I read *Moby-Dick; or, The Whale* for the first time. The kind of book that feels like a friend. The kind of book you miss when you have to be away.

Yester as unit, the unit of yester: Yesteryear, yestermonth, yesterweek, yestereve. Yesterhour yesterminute yestersecond.

I remain obsessed with Moby Dick. His "peculiar, snow-white wrinkled forehead." I know he's not real, yet it's become important: Does he know about me?

When I learned about Jesus walking on the water, I wondered if the whales gazed up and saw his feet. If Jesus didn't wear underwear they could've seen right up his robe. Later, I learned that the Sea of Galilee is only a freshwater lake.

I wasn't born yesterday.

Yesterday was Monday. Someday, when somebody reads this, that statement will be true.

When they saw Jesus walking toward them amid the wind and the waves, the disciples believed they were seeing a ghost. But Jesus told them (according to Mark, Matthew, and John), "It is I, be not afraid."

We had such happiness together / I can't believe it's gone forever. Chad is 78. Jeremy's 79. Chad has retired but Jeremy plays on.

According to Mark and Matthew, Jesus also said, "Be of good cheer!" Imagine hearing that. From Jesus. Your heart becoming a prancing deer.

On a map this morning, I saw an actual Memory Lane.

Luke never wrote anything about the incident at all. What became of all of them?

Like Baruch said in his little section of the Bible, "Where are the princes of the nations, and those who rule over the beasts on earth; those who mock the birds of the air, and who hoard up silver and gold, in which men trust, and there is no end to their getting; those who scheme to get silver, and are anxious, whose labors are beyond measure? They have vanished and gone below, and others have arisen in their place."

Don't forget: forgetting is a proven coping mechanism.

Mais où sont les neiges d'antan, goddammit? Villon was a criminal, but he asked the best question.

THE NATURAL AGENT THAT STIMULATES SIGHT AND MAKES THINGS VISIBLE

It's possible to light a candle *and* curse the darkness.

The scarlet tanager is a bird so bright it appears to emanate its own red light.

Like light itself, the word *light* alights in different forms: noun or verb or adjective accordingly.

A velvet green seascape bathed in light. A shrewd light in his eyes, the lightest blue. Light on her feet on the lawn in a light dress.

At the end of the tunnel, another tunnel. The cold light of day. It could be worse; in outer space it's always night.

I love the way, since 1986, that Tom Bodett has promised, "I'm Tom Bodett for Motel 6, and we'll leave the light on for you."

On the first day, God said, "Let there be light." On the fourth, like some kind of demented hobbyist, back he came and did some more: "Let there be lights in the firmament of the heaven to divide the day from the night; and let them be for signs, and for seasons, and for days, and years."

The chiaroscuro in Rembrandt's portraits! Every head depicted in a partial eclipse, every nose a-thrust between a dawn-like flood and a brooding dusk.

In Latin, as an adjective, Lucifer means *light-bringing*. Satan before he fell. Wild how a devil is just an angel in hell.

Emanata are squiggles scribbled on the air, emanating from a character to indicate a state: a sweat drop for anxiety, a question mark for confusion, a ray of light coming out of the sun.

Lucifer is sometimes depicted as a wingèd child pouring light from a jar, an evocation of his name as a noun: *morning star*.

I long to sit with you on a small balcony outside a French window and watch as the sunset abets your face.

In Germany, in 2017, a couple wanted to name their baby boy Lucifer, but were denied by the registrar.

Global warming forces a certain wrongness upon the sun: a chandelier hung too close to the ground.

In the 1400s, Alphonso de Spina wrote that one-third of all angels sided with Lucifer's revolt, meaning the number of demons in existence was 133,316,666. (He arrived at this figure through an exegesis of Revelations.)

In the 1500s, Johann Weyer set the figure at 4,439,622, broken down into 666 legions of 6,666 demons apiece, presided over by 66 infernal kings, accursed princes, hellish dukes, and so forth.

Demons can take on any appearance they desire, from an angel of light to President of the United States.

Buffoons by the light of the moon are still buffoons.

Matthew called Jesus the way, the truth, and the light.

According to Supreme Court Justice Louis Brandeis, "Publicity is justly commended as a remedy for social and industrial diseases. Sunlight is said to be the best of disinfectants; electric light the most efficient policeman." But no matter how many facts are brought to light, the worst of us get off without even the lightest sentence.

Will we ever again feel lighter than air? Lately I long to be out like a light.

Is this light verse? Is this light comedy? Am I doing this right?

Do you think we can make it to the city lights? The lights go down; the audience quiets.

Somebody please put a light in the window.

Seriously asking: anybody got a light?

WITH THE FACE TO THE REAR, IN THE DIRECTION BEHIND

The last day of April, showers and all. A clammy rain that's less than refreshing. Water wrung from a mildewed sponge.

The fog slips the city into a dress made of gauze. Wildlife plops itself onto lawns.

Bunnies, bunnies everywhere! Like big plump hopping loaves of bread.

Like children we crave people to examine our wounds. Like Christ we show our wounds reluctantly to doubters.

How to restore the balance of the four humors? How to choose a life and not just settle for one?

Every morning I wake up and the first person I see says, "Hi, I'm the Internet, here to shorten your memory."

Moloch demands his daily flesh. I mean the surveillance capitalism complex.

How tired am I of this plaguey empire! But it was like this when we got here.

Chittering squirrels hide nuts with alacrity, the faster to forget where they put them, perhaps.

How do the robins know when to come back?

Everyone talks about progress; no one talks about retrenchment.

Downwardly mobile—any of us could be.

Jeremiah was tasked to prophesy the destruction of a kingdom, but everyone hates that.

Denial is a popular first response to a plague.

The laws of nature could care less whether we believe in them or not.

To pronounce that things will work out as the older generation dies off is a pernicious psychosis. The widespread idea of passive advancement is just something to repeat in a lazy way.

Don't get me wrong—I, too, long to believe that everything is governed by some kind of invisible, all-pervading intelligence.

Wash your hands, wash your hearts.

What does *Nessun dorma* even mean? *Let no one sleep.* At the end of the day, sleep slurps me up.

I used to fantasize that if I lost my job, then I'd open up a roller rink. My new career change fantasy is religious mystic. Dorothy Day style. Passion and conviction and maddening contradiction living totally outside the conventions of society. To be flypaper for freaks and to love them all equally.

Why is it so hard to do something heroic straightforwardly? Stealing a hoard of diamonds from the wealthy and redistributing them? A simple morality, no ambiguity.

Would that the 21st Century so far were a tweet, one that we could delete forever.

The world was already sick to begin with. A corporate fantasia. A money-blasted hellscape. A near dystopia unto death where Orlando is routinely less warm than Antarctica.

It's bad, okay, but die another day, why don't you? (I said that to myself.)

In Norway, they personified the plague as a hag, a bent old woman clad in a black hood, carrying a broom and a rake. If she used the broom, all souls in the area were doomed, but if she used the rake, some might escape through the teeth.

Labor of love, labor of lunacy. In chaos might we find a new future?

The surgical removal of evil from the corpus of the world.

What do you think Malcolm X meant by "by any means necessary"?

All we need is drastic action coupled with strong will. And maybe a miraculous event, unforeseen.

We must do more than idly talk. We must become a flock of smaller birds attacking a hawk.

ACKNOWLEDGMENTS

Much gratitude to the editors of the publications in which many of these pieces originally appeared, sometimes in slightly different form, including:

"*Ubi Sunt*" and "The Natural Agent that Stimulates Sight and Makes Things Visible" in *Always Crashing*

"A Quiet State After Some Period of Disturbance" and "Exalted or Worthy of Complete Devotion" in *Another Chicago Magazine*

"To Celebrate the Anniversary of Someone's Birth" (as "Birthday") in *The Atlantic*

"The Sweet and Fleshy Product of a Tree or Other Plant" in *Brevity*

"One Authorized to Perform the Sacred Rites" and "A Source of Inspiration, a Guiding Genius" in *Cimarron Review*

"Foretelling the Future by a Randomly Chosen Passage from a Book" and "The State or Period of Being a Child" in *Court Green*

"The Word by Which a Person or Thing is Denoted," "A Human Female Who Has Given Birth to a Baby," and "To Cherish a Desire with Anticipation" in *DIAGRAM*

"A Power or Ability of the Kind Possessed by Superheroes" in *Heavy Feather Review*

"The Moon Is the Moon Whether We Call It That Or Not," "A Talisman Attracts, an Amulet Repels," and "Hump Day Has Always Been a Terrible Nickname" in *New World Writing*

"To Replicate the Sacrifice of Christ's Journey into the Desert for 40 Days" in *NOON: Journal of the Short Poem*

"The Special Organ of Breathing and Smelling" in *North American Review*

"Ekphrastic" and "A Building That Serves as Living Quarters" in *Puerto del Sol*

"The Ten of Pentacles" in *RHINO*

"How to Act" on The Runaways Lab Theatre website

"The Physical Universe Beyond the Earth's Atmosphere," "The Act of Passing Across or Through," and A Place Set Aside for Burial of the Dead" in *Sporklet*

"With the Face to the Rear, in the Direction Behind" in *TriQuarterly*

"The Production and Consumption of Goods and Services" and "Pastoral" in *Women's Review of Books*.

"The Moon Is the Moon Whether We Call It That or Not" also appears in *The Lunar Codex* anthology, archived in a time capsule placed on the Moon in November of 2021; "Foretelling the Future by a Randomly Chosen Passage from a Book" appears in the limited-edition chapbook *Fruit Bat Press Presents: A Very Chicago December* published in December 2021; and "Birthday" was featured on the podcast *The Slowdown* hosted by Ada Limón in 2021.

Appreciation beyond measure to Kimberly Southwick-Thompson, poet, editor, and friend extraordinaire, who put together a poem-a-day group in April of 2020, creating a community of people working together on a common cause. The earliest drafts of the poems that became this manuscript originated there and for that opportunity and encouragement, I will be forever grateful. Thanks, too, to all my fellow group members, especially Jose Hernandez Diaz, Tyler Gillespie, Patrick Holian, and Tova Kranz.

Huge thanks to Kazim Ali for selecting this manuscript from a mountain of worthy ones, and to everyone at Texas Review Press for making gorgeous books and getting them out into the world.

Thanks as well to the city of Chicago and the generosity of its literary community. And very particular thanks to Jessica Anne, Lisa Bankoff, Abby Beckel, Logan Berry, Kim Brooks, Sommer Browning, Eileen Colwell, Sarah Dodson, Julia Fine, Virginia Konchan, Caro Macon Fleischer, Elisa Gabbert, Aviya Kushner, Ananda Lima, Timothy Moore, José Olivarez, Eric Plattner, Robert Puccinelli, David Renka, Beth Rooney, Martin Seay, Rachel Slotnick, Will Stone, Rose Super and Luka Super, Marcus Wicker; my family, but especially my parents; all the poets who do and have ever done Poems While You Wait; my students and colleagues at DePaul University; and anyone who has ever talked with me about this world and its absurdity and beauty.